Awakening of the Heart

To Vincent,
my love
The one who
awakened
my heart -
I love you,
I always will ♡
Barbara
x

Also by Barbara Gianquitto

4:04AM Thoughts

Awakening of the Heart

POETRY AND PROSE BY
BARBARA GIANQUITTO

Awakening of the Heart

ISBN 978-1-7395880-0-7

Illustrations and cover by: Elizabeth Spary

Editor: Stefanie Briar

To Elisabetta and Erica

May your hearts always

bloom in love

Contents

Introduction

I'm not here to preach, I am not here to teach.
I am here to tell you my story:
the pain I have been through,
the battles I've endured,
the tears that those eyes have been home to.
It would have been easier to give up,
to give in,
to blend into the darkness and make a nest,
to feed the monsters gripping my neck
during every anxiety attack that invaded my body.

I believed every word of unworthiness for years.
I believed my vulnerability was a weakness,
stripped down to my bones,
exposed like trees in cold winter:
left there for the wolves to feast on, feeding them insecurities like snacks.
I didn't recognise my face in the mirror;
I saw a stranger, I had to make her acquaintance again.
Numb to everything, I moved like a ragdoll, limbs too heavy to carry around,
afraid to smile as even the air hitting my teeth was too painful to bear.
Aching in places I never even knew existed.

I believed every word, for so long. I'd never amount to anything, I'd never be good enough, what I was chasing was just a childlike idiotic dream.
I had to force my eyes open and finally say 'enough'.

I was always alone, even before I decided to be alone,
and that was the beginning of my awakening:
the awakening of my heart.

Heartbreak and pain have been my ticket to finally embark on my own journey of healing and understanding. It's one I had to take alone.
I finally realised I used to hold my happiness hostage, measuring it by my ability to make someone else happy. My worth was defined by the level of love I received.
So when it all went away, I felt broken, unlovable, and unworthy.
I learned to slowly accept myself for who I had become.
I learned that 'No' doesn't require any apologies.
That I can choose otherwise, and that I don't have to tolerate things out of fear that people would leave me.
That I didn't have to try so hard to be accepted by others, and that the real work is inside.

Today I walk with more confidence, I listen to my intuition, I believe in myself a little bit more every day, I'm walking the walk, and I'm doing the work.
I look back with sweet melancholy, wishing I had been kinder with myself.

This book is a raw and unfiltered collection of poems and prose from the deepest heartbreak into finding, trusting, and loving myself again; learning how to stay soft in a world that kept battering my hopes and dreams; about life and the cycle of love, the ups and downs of an incredibly non-linear healing. It's about finding love again, wearing scars around my neck like pearls, and following my intuition as a sacred spell I cast upon myself.
It's about no longer being afraid to show up exactly as I am, as I have become; with wisdom in my pockets and a heart that is larger than life.

I am not here to preach; I am not here to teach.

I am here to tell you my story.

For the truth seekers

and deep thinkers,

For the hopeless romantics

in love with love,

For hearts larger than life

ready to reclaim their power.

For the once lost,

Part I

The Circle of Sorrow

Will it be home again?

I am sitting on my breastfeeding chair completely paralyzed. I have used this chair for so long. I have fallen asleep with my baby on this chair,
I have held them both and fed them to sleep.
I have cuddled them and watched those innocent eyes falling asleep in my arms. What am I going to do with this chair? How can I pack this?
Where have I gone wrong?
The hopes and dreams.
The pregnancies, the happiness of having another baby.
The trips abroad and the laughter.
Standing in front of all our pictures and feeling the tears burning my face.
The first day at school, the first baby laughter snapped in an eternal picture. Completely overwhelmed.
I am packing away my life. My life as I know it. All I have ever had, now in boxes, labelled with a black marker, ready to go into a new house.
Will it be a home?
Will I be happy again?
Will I feel whole again?
How did we get here?
How do you move on?
How do you start all over again?

How do you believe again?
Am I worthy of happiness?
Am I worthy of love?

Unspoken words

The sound of these unspoken words is deafening.
Silent words weep from the walls around us,
flying around the room
like knives ready to cut,
like shards ready to place themselves
in the chambers of our hearts.
Yet, we don't give them the oxygen
to come alive.
If we did, the cuts would be too deep.
So, we leave them in the
only place we can:
Between my last deep sigh
and your next breath.

Running towards fear

If I ran towards fear,
I'd stumble and fall.
I'd hurt myself even more
than if I stayed in this stillness.
If I ran towards fear,
the oxygen would wear thin,
my lungs would scream,
my heart would shatter even more.
So, I stay where I am,
unable to move forward,
impossible to go back.
Nothingness around me,
I want to fly away and leave it all behind.
My fingernails sink deep into the ground,
I look down.
I stay down.
Nobody is here.
Nobody is pulling me up.
I need to do it myself.

Images

I was stuck in an image
of whom you wanted me to be.

What a tragedy that my longing for love
was greater than your ability
to see me for who I really was.

Hunger

Eating bread whilst filling up on hunger,
that's what your love felt like:
starving my aching heart,
replacing my hunger for love
with a plate full of lies.
Day by day,
you shattered all illusions,
a love that was only there to take,
leaving breadcrumbs behind
so I could always find my way back
to a castle built on illusions,
Starving to the point of non-recognition.
Eating bread whilst filling up on hunger,
that's what your love felt like.

Set me free

Possessiveness and control
cannot be justified
in the name of love.
Love should set us
free.

Letting go

Tonight I don't want to be strong,
I want to be soft and vulnerable and just want to be held,
strong and tight in a way I know I won't break, because you won't hurt me.
I want to be saved and I don't want to feel ashamed
or feel less of a strong woman for wanting so.
I don't want to be Wonder Woman tonight,
running a house, single mum, working full time.
No. Tonight I want to be just a girl, no thoughts, no responsibilities.
I want to forget that I am 40 years old, divorced and lonely.
I want to be okay with being fiercely independent and still saying "I miss you".
I want to melt in your arms and just breathe,
breathe until my heart slows down, as it does when I feel safe.
Tonight, I want to return to softness and love and warm feelings,
I want to ditch any logic.
Can we do that?

Crying all my tears

I am crying all the tears that I held
for every time I was too proud to ask for help,
too proud to say I am not okay,
too proud to tell you I miss you like hell,
too stubborn to stop and breathe.
I cried the tears that needed to be cried,
like you're collapsing on yourself in a ball and you feel like the world is against you.
They say to welcome sadness, acknowledge it, feel it,
duck under the wave and wait until it passes.
I am crying for all the love lost,
for all the love that could have been and all the love I couldn't have,
all the love that has been ripped out of me, when I had no choice,
for all the love I couldn't give and all the love I didn't receive.
It's like a breakthrough, the longest and darkest night before the dawn.

Shooting star

Another shooting star
has come and gone,
brightening the sky in such a way
that I forgot the darkness of the night.

Why does the stardust surrounding me
feel more like ashes falling from the sky?

I need to stop

I need to stop walking into the raging fires
hoping I won't get burned,
as if they were friendly flames.
A flame is a flame:
burning is what it's supposed to do.
As much as they look attractive and hot,
it's not flames I should be chasing,
but rainbows, wildflowers, and cups of peppermint tea.
I won't dance in the fire this time;
I will watch from a distance
waiting until the embers burn out.
I will say goodbye to the ashes
as they are eclipsed by a warm summer breeze.

Purple

My favourite colour makes me think of lavender and spring,
of a sunny day walking in a field of sunflowers and lavender.
If I close my eyes, I can feel the sun kissing my nose and my
heart slowing down, each heartbeat in sync with my blood:
slower.
Peaceful.

I can smell the flowers, and remember for the first time in such
a long time what it feels like to be carefree.
And now my mouth is strangely moving, what is this?
A smile?

Do you remember smiling?

Up until now, purple was the colour of the rain (as the song
goes), my heart has been closed, used, abused, made fun of,
filled with lies and absurdities.
My mind is racing to try and understand what exactly you were
saying, trying to box me off in some sort of strange reality I
am not going to sign up for.

Purple rain drenches me in disappointment, in unmet expectations and games.
My feelings were not a game!
I hope you had your fun crushing down hopes and dreams.

But there will be no more purple rain.

I know where I stand now, and I will not apologise for wanting to live my life as I wish, for asking for the love I deserve instead of saying thank you for breadcrumbs, just because, hey, *you fed me, after all.*

I'm not sorry for wanting to run like a reckless child in a field of lavender flowers, and filling my belly with laughter.

Do you remember laughing?

The winter in my heart is ending soon;
I will not allow you to bring misery to my life once again.
You may dress it up with fancy words of the eternal love
that never quite matched your actions.

Purple is the colour of my soul, and it is pure and beautiful.
It is something you will never comprehend.
I'm letting everything go.
It's just me now, and I will be enough for myself.

I will inhale happiness, exhale grief.

Grieving

I grieve the image of a tomorrow
that never came,
all the ways you could have loved me
and all the reasons why you couldn't.

I don't fit

I don't fit. I just don't fit with this world sometimes.
I feel like an alien, looking people in their eyes and waiting for them to give a human response that makes sense.
Who is the alien I wonder, me or them?
Their language feels absurd to me, their actions confusing,
I'm tired of second guessing all the time: it is exhausting.
The air is stale like old bread, my heart heavy like a rock in the ocean, constantly attacked by waves, relentless.
Sometimes I just feel it would be easier to simply surrender, stop expecting anything.
I vowed I wouldn't become a bitter old soul, but life is testing me.
I always thought there is a lesson in everything and that the universe keeps offering the same lesson until it is learnt.
But I am tired of pushing things forward,
trying every day and doing the work. Today I don't want to.
I want to feel miserable and sorry for myself, that must be allowed, is it not?
I just don't fit in a strange world of instant gratification, distance and silence.

You can't tame me

You can't tame this wild heart.
The fire inside has been burning
since the
beginning
of
    time.

Darkness

The path is not paved,
the branches are shaking.
The wolf's eyes are deep,
penetrating my soul.
I hold my breath when all I want to do
is to give in.
I am not afraid of the absence of light.
I've never seen more clearly
than in this
    darkness.

Not what you ordered

You waltzed into my life like walking into a restaurant,
after having read the menu and all the reviews.
Charming place, delicious plates, at least from the pictures it looked amazing.
Surely you would love the specials on the menu.
A bit exotic in flavours and combinations of ingredients, but it looked and sounded like you would absolutely love it.
The dish arrived, excitement pouring out of every fibre of your being.
Then the disappointment, you don't like the taste of it.
Is it the texture, the presentation?
Is it too hot or too cold?
Your brain is rattling, trying to find an explanation for such unmet expectations.
You take a bite.
What to do now? This is not what you thought it would taste like.
The restaurant is so fancy, music is playing, wine is flowing.
And you are absolutely starving.
Should you take another bite?
Should you try to reason with yourself that there is nothing not to like?
What's wrong with you?

And the eternal debate starts in your mind, how can you not like something you were absolutely sure you would like?
No amount of logic can affect your tastebuds.
Maybe you should order something else.

What if?

What if I didn't want to
let you go?
What if I wanted to hold on
to us?
Would my heart be strong enough
for the both of us?

Versions of me

You don't miss me.
You miss a version of me
you created it in your head.
I can't even attempt to bridge that g a p.
I don't even know who she is.

I loved you

I loved you hungrily,
hurrying to feel skin-deep touch
and soul connection.
I loved you when the full moon first shone on us,
in the dark,
in the silence of your deep eyes.
Somewhere between longing and illusion,
I worshipped the image of you,
like a new religion,
before I even knew what your soul was made of.
I loved you like a tempest in winter:
mercilessly and furiously,
setting the world on fire
into a hurricane of passion,
giving into the magnetic pull,
making the ground shake and somehow feeling like
I had a grip.
I loved you until the Earth split open
and the sky broke into ashes,
swallowing what was left of us:
The ultimate sacrifice to a God
I don't believe in.

The last time

The last time I said
'I love you',
you held me tight in your arms.
It wasn't just some letters
tossed together.
It was a calling,
an essence,
a beacon.
It was my heart,
right there
in words.

Wasted love?

My heart can hardly contain these feelings.
They spill out of its chambers
like water coming out from an overflowing pool.
Thousands of drops now re-absorb into the earth,
giving way to different roots.

Wasted love or new beginnings?

Unburnt

Watch me float away
like a beautiful dream you can't hold on to.
Watch me walk confidently
away from the flames:
unburnt,
unscathed,
unbroken,
because the only things broken
are your promises.
I never needed your love,
but I sure as hell deserved
your respect.

'What can I do to help?'

There is nothing you can do to help me,
unless you can become my slow breath
and rhythmic heartbeat,
my sleep and peaceful dreams.
A clear mind,
taking all the clutter and burning it
with old wood into a campfire.
Unless you can become the breeze of wind
that whispers words of wisdom,
instead of terrifying sounds.
Unless you can become the Earth
I can safely walk barefoot on,
the calm river I can bathe my sins in,
the Holy Grail of clarity
and peace.

How dare you?

How dare you reappear like this?
What do I do now with all these feelings?
Waves, oceans of emotions are submerging me,
trying to rip open my stone heart
and pour love and sweet, warm honey in it.
This heart of mine
closed shut the last time we said goodbye.
Your sweet words are not cutting it,
and yet, once again, through all lifetimes
you are still the only one
who can even barely attempt to make me listen.

Crumbs

I have been holding on to pieces,
blindly following the trails
of crumbs.
Tiptoeing on broken glass,
and you kept calling it
        'love'.

Those stars

Does it still hurt?
What happened to all our promises and all the forever?
Tell me, does it still hurt
to think of me?
I try not to think of us,
as I walk in the cold morning breeze.
I couldn't save you,
I couldn't save us.
I am moving forward and you're not with me.
Tell me, does it still hurt?
I used to whisper your name like an exhale,
a prayer.
When did it become such a curse?
My mind wanders,
longing to curl up in your arms once more,
if I could just erase the pain
and replace the ashes with flowers.
Maybe,
oh maybe I could...
but I know,
I know you're far away.
You are in those stars
we could never rewrite
after all.

Through the noise

You wanted the movie love scenes.
I wanted you in real life,
with the kids making noise,
holding my hand in the car.

Feelings are valid

It's okay if you don't understand me.
My feelings aren't less valid
because of it.

She is afraid

She is afraid of the light in the dark.
She is petrified of salvation and redemption,
for her sins to be washed.
Light means to open up and she knows what happens
when she does.
Better stay in the dark, it can't get any worse than that.
She knows,
yes, she knows.
Words don't mean much,
it's the silence she craves.
In the dark,
silence is all there is.

Dark love

I love you like
all dark things
should be loved...
from a great
d i s t a n c e.

The puppet and the master

Every time we get close, we collide.
Melting in a field of passion and love,
I get burned again and you retreat,
in silence,
just enough for the scabs to form on my burnt flesh.
Then you return,
luring me back with sweet words
and promises of forever.
You were always the master,
moving me exactly
where you wanted me to be.
As if it was always my choice,
hiding the strings of the puppet
so skilfully.
I don't want to play anymore.
I am my own master
and I don't play with monsters.
Not anymore.
I am b r e a k i n g free.

Shutting down

I am waiting,
but I am tired of waiting.
I am hoping,
but I am tired of hoping.
I feel like shutting down the world.
Will you hold me as I quietly crumble,
just for a little while?

Deafening silence

In the eternal dance of flames,
ethereal words that never came
left us in a limbo of hopes,
that vanishes more and more each day.
All in the name of fear,
everything for the sake of pride.
So much left undone,
too much remains unsaid.
Of all the unspoken words,
yours were the loudest.

Painfully simple

Sometimes things are just
painfully simple.
Raise the bar, beautiful soul,
little ants won't be able
to crawl over it.

Chasing an image

How can I miss something
I never had?
Or am I missing the images
of a future that never happened?
Why do I do that?
Why do you allow it?

I break things

I break things that are beautiful and pure
because I can't trust them.
I can't trust what is given to me because it always
gets taken away.
At what point did I learn that it is better to destroy than to build?
Where has the innocence gone?
Where is the magic?
Where are the fairies hiding?

Unbreakable

No amount of words
can penetrate this soul
enough to make me believe
I am not worthy.
You cannot sew a dress on me
and ask me to wear it
as if I had chosen it.

Burn

And if we have to burn,
let it be an explosion so big
that it lights the entire universe.
Let it be a combustion of hearts and minds,
let it be the creation of a new galaxy
named after us.
Nobody will ever know the pain
behind the shining new stars.
Let them be the immortal memories
of the greatest love
that
never
was.

Understanding and forgiveness

Don't confuse my kindness
for foolishness.
Understanding and forgiveness
are
two
different
things.

Chaos

You were the chaos
  that made
    the most sense.

Unmasked

I want to fill this silence
with the sound of my tears.
I want to finally let go,
become undone
unzipped, unmasked.
See me for what I really am.
Tell me,
do you still love me?

Energy

I could always feel
every atom of energy
changing between us.
Even before you
could realise it.
It has always been my
greatest gift,
and my biggest
        curse.

Always you

If I could have one last choice,
it would always be you, my love.
I will always choose you
in every dream,
in every realm,
in every sigh,
in every breath.

If not in this life,
then in the next.

Miss you

I miss you;
  I always do.
I just never allow
  myself to think of you.
I wouldn't be able
  to say goodbye
    again.

Bees

So, is it *goodbye* already?
Or was it even *hello*?
Thought it was a pot of gold,
shame it was simply
a hive of bees.

Too complex

I'm too complex for you,
I'm too complex for me,
I'm too complex for this world.
You can try,
  try
      try...
to listen, to understand,
to love me.
Will it ever be enough
for my wandering soul?

Phases

The only phases I follow
are the Moon's.
Not Love's.
Love is either there or it isn't.
And if it comes in phases,
it is not
  for
    me.

We were wrong

There was Love,
outpouring from every fibre,
like a river overflowing.
As if Love itself recognised that
it was right.
I guess we were all
wrong.

I let you go

I let you go
like I never wanted anybody to go:
piece by piece,
tear by tear
memory by memory.

Come close

Hold me between breaths and sheets.
Let me open my mouth to drink you in,
sink into my veins
quickly like poison,
whilst making my pulse raging
as if it were about to explode.
Pull me into heaven,
let me surrender to the sweet memory
of your skilful touch
and sinful mouth,
before returning to the hell
of a world without you.

Seeing you go

There is almost a sense of impossibility
in seeing you go,
like a wave leaving the shore.

Dark sky

He was water in a sandy desert,
fresh as strawberries picked on a hot summer day,
calming the raging storm my heart was drowning to,
tiptoeing around me like a gentle dance
my body couldn't resist moving to.
A shelter of hopes and dreams my heart opened towards.
The sky brightened for a fleeting moment,
like a shooting star,
making me forget that the sky
was still dark
after all.

Trapped

I hate being trapped in this idea you have of me.
It's like a padlock without a key.
For there is no escape
but to try and live up
to impossible expectations.

Mirrors of time

I am afraid of the coldness my soul is in.
I keep looking for the fire,
for the light
for the warmth.
For the soul companion I lost eons ago
in a heart-shattering loss.
I cannot rest until I find you again.
I keep looking in the woods,
in the forests,
in the remote corners of the Universe,
in the black holes of the mirrors of Time.
Painfully and frantically searching,
like I promised you,
in the last words that left my dying breath.
This ache transcends time and space,
it has no logic.
And every time I think I found you
and life reminds me that I was wrong –
I lose you
all
over
again.

Answers

You were my answer,
you were all my answers.
I just was never
your question.

Part II

The Rite of Passage

Aren't you tired yet?

Aren't you tired yet
of this life full of lies and doubts
being second-guessed and taken for granted?

Aren't you tired yet
of putting a mask on and faking a smile
when all you want to do is to crumble?

Aren't you tired yet
of saying 'yes, I'll work on it' when really
the only thing you should be working on
is enforcing your own boundaries?

Because saying 'No' does not require apologies.

Being you, and being proud of who you are,
does not require any validation.

Tell me, aren't you tired yet
of trying to fit in a world of chaos,
of listening to what people say you should be?

Because your heart has already known grief,
loss and betrayal and it is now your time to shine.
Step out of the shadows and embrace who you are,
because you are wonderful and everything

this world needs more of.

Tell me,
aren't you tired yet
of not believing any of this?

Close the door

Close the door,
open the windows,
burn some sage,
let the music beat in sync with
your heart.
Slow down.
Breathe,
breathe some more.
Let the tears cleanse your soul.
Take stock;
sometimes stillness
is the only progress
we need.

Gold temple

I went to see the shaman today.
We talked about a fish and a pond too small for her,
about a bluebird ready to fly away
with its empty beauty.
About death that never dies,
and life that always lives.
About a black swan navigating calm waters,
and a little girl who lost everything she ever loved.
We talked about cherry trees and oak roots,
of letting go and making space for new energy.
For love and trust,
dipping myself in gold in an ancient temple.
Reminding me of what my worth
always was.

Remember

Remember my love,
there is a rainbow
on the other side of
fear.
Breathe;
the only way is
forward.

Magic

I believe in magic.
In the magic of listening to one another,
not just hearing the words,
but in the attempt to truly understand one another.
In those moments when nothing really makes sense,
when screaming would be easier,
where running away feels like the only option.
Magic is found in stillness.
Breathe,
  listen,
    repeat.

Keep rising

And I will keep rising
and walking uphill,
alone but strong.
Nobody will drag me down
in the streets of self-doubt again.
A broken heart is heavier to carry,
but I choose freedom over a cage
made of illusions and broken promises.

Stillness

The gentle movement of the sea
is cocooning me like a gentle embrace.
Hot coffee and light heart,
I have never felt so grounded
like in the middle of the
    sea.

Roots

There is a longing in my heart,
a deeply-rooted desire for silence
and inner peace,
to surrender to the gentle breeze
of change
whilst grounding myself more and more
with newfound roots
into the depths of my
ever-wandering soul.

Moving forward

I met an old version of me.
I recognised her;
the chaos felt familiar.
It was almost an invitation to step back.
I just have to remind her
of how far she has come.
Just a few more layers to shed,
to break the chains of the past,
of ancient beliefs and systems.
They have to remain with the old version.
She is moving
forward.

Dreams

I dream in colours of longing
and shades of
impossibilities.

Free spirit

I used to think that I had to live my life in a certain way,
obey certain rules,
because that's what everyone did.
Or that's what the norm was.
I kept trying to fit into certain schemes and images
that the world had of me.
Always somehow feeling unsettled,
restless, anxious, and caged.
I realised I wasn't meant for a world that defines me,
that wants me to play by its rules.
I want to define the world with my own beliefs.
Because after all the years trying to tell myself otherwise,
I now know that I am a free spirit:
always have been, always will be,
and free spirits cannot be caged.
They will try to escape even through
the bar of a rhyme.

Just feel it

Maybe the point is to just feel.
Feel it all.
In your bones.
In every fibre of your being.
Don't resist it,
feel it all.
Even if that means
allowing your heart
to break fully.

Fly away with me

I refuse to live in fear.
I release all doubts and chains, I'm tired of leaving it all to chance.
I am grabbing life by the horns, I will make it happen.
Whatever it is my heart is longing for.
Whatever it is my soul is craving.
I don't know how many lives we have,
if I will remember this one when I step into the next realm.
But when all is said and done, when the chips are down and the flames are extinguishing, I want to say 'I have lived'.
To the fullest, with integrity, true to myself and what I stand for.
And I stand with the truth, with love.
Soft, open, alive.
I want to fly away, free and happy.
You can fly with me for a while, or for longer.
But fly with me, not around me or behind me.
Feel the wind and the freedom, and when you want to rest, feel free to take a breath.
But don't look back.
That's progress, that's the journey to happiness.
Fly with me, or not.

I am going anyway.

Lost and found

I am feeling lost and found,
all at the same time,
in a space where I can be broken
and whole,
where I can have everything
whilst wanting
nothing.
It's quiet, it's warm and comforting.
It calms the storm of emotions.
The soft breeze of spring is caressing
my cheeks like a soft hug,
reminding me to be present in the now.
It's okay if I don't know.
It is simply okay.
Nobody has it all figured out.

Be You

Be your authentic, beautiful self.
Everything will follow,
even if that means
losing people along the journey.

Sacred intuition

I am finally comfortable in my own skin,
not afraid to show my bare soul.
I wear my scars like pearls around my neck,
I feel free as a river.
Like the moon I now follow my own phases,
I retreat when it's time to rest
and shine when I am ready to.
I follow my intuition like a sacred spell
I cast upon myself.

Full Moon

The energy of the full moon is calling.
It is so powerful,
it is inviting me to step out
of the darkness
to shine in my own full light.
My time is
now.

Through the shadows

Go through the shadows,
go where it is uncomfortable,
feel the pain,
the one that rips you open.
Allow your heart to break fully,
the light will finally filter through there.

Respect and kindness

Respect and kindness are human rights,
not privileges.

Did you forget?

You have been amazing before.
You have simply forgotten
how great you were.
I am here to remind you,
so you can let that fire out again.
Burn,
  inspire,
    fly,
      soar.

Rest

Rest your aching bones,
breathe in the wind of change.
Surrender to the unknown.
Everything will soon
make sense.

My soul

I am no longer interested
in anything that
does not feed
my soul.

Earth roots

Today I return to the roots,
  to the beginning,
    deep into the earth,
      within the fire of the centre.
There is space there to breathe,
  my lungs are accustomed to
    the flames.
The earth is cocooning me,
  limbs fusing into the fire,
    not burning, just finally
      b r e a t h i n g.

Happiness

The only thing I'm ever
going to chase from now on
is my own
            happiness.

Fighter

You look like someone
who has survived
the biggest storms
and toughest battles.
Yet, you are still smiling,
you are still standing,
you are still living,
you are still loving.

Just wait

Some questions are not revealed
until the answers arrive.

Un-learning

I am learning to
'un-learn'
slowly and painfully,
but oh,
it is so empowering.

The silence within

I am making space
for the silence within.
Finally vibrating higher
and authentically.
Which feels a lot
like simply
saying
'no'.

Honey and lavender

I am honey and lavender,
a delicate scent only for
your nostrils.
Don't be fooled by the
delicate colours of my soul,
for I have known loss and grief.
My heart has been lost
so many times before,
each piece shattered,
never quite returned.
But I choose to return to softness
and an open heart,
to breathe positivity and walk with confidence,
alone.
Greatness awaits me.
I know it.

Light and darkness

I embrace the periods
of darkness with grace,
I accept with gratitude
the soft energy of the shadows.
The moon, after all,
shines in the
                dark.

Lifetimes

Sometimes I feel like a child,
just beginning to grow.
Innocence mixed with experience,
insatiable curiosity,
and outpouring energy
deeply rooted into the universe,
where my soul keeps on travelling
between now and forever:
exploring, growing
healing,
attempting to fulfil what this
body was always meant to do this lifetime.

Fire in you

The fire in you
was never meant
to be tamed.
Those flames are
meant to light
the
    world.

I am a Yes

I am an answer,
not a question.
I am a certainty,
not a doubt.
You hear me?
I am a 'Yes'
    not
        a
          'maybe'.

Summer

The summer is made for
shedding old skin
and ancient beliefs,
for long naps to restore energy,
kisses, and tight hugs.
Summer is for returning to laughter
and feeling light,
finding happiness in
fresh strawberries just picked,
whilst the sun warms
our hearts.
Summer feels a lot like
  coming
    home.

Never settling

I am a mixture of chaos and art,
of fire and ice,
of lavender and oak tree,
mostly ungrounded,
constantly dreaming,
forever questioning,
never settling.

Growth

The moments of growth
are the most unsettling, even painful.
It feels like you are lost,
ungrounded, with no clarity.
The new direction is only hidden
in the fog that surrounds you.
I know it's scary to trust the process,
but stay with it.

Over-Love

I over-think,
over-talk,
over-feel,
and over-love
and that is

absolutely beautiful.

Your soul has a voice

Stay still and quiet,
let it come to you.
Feel your body, your muscles,
your hair, your feet on the ground.
feel the energy moving in and
through your body.
Listen calmly,
your soul has a voice:
a voice that is louder in total silence.

Time

I need time,
space
and suffocating hugs
all at once.

Do more

If you want more love,
give more love.
If you want to be heard,
do more listening.
If you want more connection,
connect more.
Do more.
Give more.
Do what you need more of,
and watch the energy start changing.

Wonderfully You

You are not damaged,
you are scarred.
You are not broken,
you are healing.
You are not 'too much';
you are everything
this world needs
more
of.

No apologies

I make no apologies
for being who I am,
not anymore.
I worked too hard to free myself
from the chains
this world had placed
around me.

Made for the wild

I was made for the wild,
to fly high and free
side by side with
the birds, across the skies,
through the trees,
dissolving into the wind
and everything soft.

Safe

I am every bird flying into a white sky,
every snowflake falling,
falling,
falling softly,
gently onto the ground.
I am resting on the branches of the trees;
silence today is not deafening,
it is comforting.
I can hear my breath,
my lungs expanding into new life,
contracting one last time to let go of what needs to go.
I can feel my blood rushing to my veins
as I walk on to the white grass.
I see footsteps in front of me,
many behind,
so many....
nothing else matters right now.
Just my breath.
I am safe.

The bird who flew away

And when they will ask you about me,
how I chose to live my life,
why I decided to let go of negativity,
tell them I was the bird who flew away.

Tell them my secrets were too big for
their small ears.
Tell them my heart swelled outside
of my tiny ribcage;
tell them the fire didn't tame me.

Tell them,
I was the fire
itself.

I am made of

I am made of truth and water,
of soft winds and strong roots
expanding
and contracting
like waves on shore.

Part III

The Magic of Love

To the man I haven't met yet

Tonight, I miss you.
You don't quite have a face, more like a soul-magnetic energy that I wonder if I know yet.
I'm a little melancholic as I think of you, embodying all my past loves, and all the parts that I loved and lost.

I miss you cooking for me, and making me laugh like crazy with loud music and silly dances in the kitchen.

I miss you who would ring me five times a day, and I also miss how annoyed I was at it!
I miss you who would open a bottle of wine and rub my feet, and forget about the world together, plainly, and simply
no real commitment for the future, just taking it one day at the time.

I miss you, who would wake up next to me every morning
and fall asleep every night with your arms around me,
I miss that sense of safety and, yes, routine.
I miss knowing I'll come home to you and your annoying habits.
I miss you who would talk for hours about absolutely nothing,
I miss your poignant questions about my life, and the healthy challenges about my choices, always with a smile and a safe space to talk.

I miss the future you; I know you are waiting for me.

I am writing about you lately, my next love, I imagine how you will take care of me and me, you.
How it will be effortless from the start, and how my heart will feel at peace just by you being around me.
How you will love my every contradiction, and how we will teach each other what love truly is.
How we will be connected not by trauma but by hope.
I imagine us sitting by a campfire imagining our life together, and planning, excited about it.
Without fear, without any need of running away or slowing things down, both emotionally available, at peace with our past and excited about our future.

I imagine waking up next to you and not wanting to leave the bed, but then doing it anyway, knowing that I will soon come back to you.
And our house, warm and comforting nights drinking wine and unwinding after a long day...
I often wonder where you are now... are you in your last relationship before me?
How is your heart today?

Are you scared, are you sad?

Have you learned what you had to before me?
My heart is heavy, my future love.
I keep on orbiting around stagnant energy
and old patterns that I can't seem to break.

I am scared most of the time of not being worthy, yet I empower
people in loving themselves first and foremost.
I feel anxious and empty and unfulfilled most of the time.
I am only at peace when I write and spill my emotions.

I'd love to know your name.
I'd love to know how we will meet and how we will know it's us.

But darling, I am healing, as this time I want to be ready for you.

Tell me your story

Tell me your story;
no, not what your job is or what your hobbies are.
Tell me what scares you.
Tell me about your pain.
Tell me, when did your heart last feel light?
Tell me your deepest desires,
your hopes and dreams.
Tell me about the shadows,
and what does your soul crave?
Tell me how to love you.
Sit with me,
tell me your story.

My type of love

I want a love that opens my ribcage, gets to the very core of my heart, and says 'I'm here, now, no matter what'.
I want a love that can hear the deafening sound of silence, understands how loudly I am screaming, and knows exactly how tightly I need to be held.
I want a love that consumes my every fibre, because I won't burn in the flames.
I want a love where intimacy has little to do with sex and physical contact,
the one where I don't have to second-guess and not know where I stand.
The one everyone keeps saying doesn't exist.

May your next love be

May your next love want all your tomorrows
to be theirs.
May it always make you feel free,
protected and embraced, even on days
you feel unlovable and unworthy.
May your next love claim your heart gently
and without demands.
May your next love be present and show up,
without any need of asking.
May it be effortless on most days
and cherish all your differences without using them
as reasons to run away.

May your next love be soft as a snowflake and calm as a breeze.
May it carry you gently as a feather in the wind
on days you can't even stand on your feet.
May it lull you to sleep with gentle head strokes
as you hear them saying 'Everything will be okay'
in the only place you will always call home.

May your next love make all your feelings valid.
May your heart feel at peace.
May your next love want all your tomorrows
to
be
theirs.

You

And then there was you,
a gentle breeze
after a long winter.
The answer to a question
I didn't know
I was longing for.

What is love, really?

What is love, really?
A concatenation of events,
smells, kisses, orgasms,
touches, smiles, safety?
Filling the gaps?
The longing?
A chemical reaction?
A hook?
Is it the damnation or the redemption?
The drug or the medicine?
The high or the low?
Or is it everything whilst we find reasons to say it's nothing?
What is love, really?
One look at you, and I can't breathe,
you bring me to my knees,
defenceless.
Do I really have a choice?
Do WE really have a choice?

The biggest love

I used to write about the big things
big feelings, big loves, big heartbreaks.
Now I write about how my fingers get trapped in your knotty hair
that you refused to brush this morning.
I write about how I trace your back bones with my fingers
as you fall asleep.
How your head rests perfectly on my chest and,
as I look down,
I fall in love with every inch of you, more and more each day.
With you long eyelashes and how you fall asleep with your mouth slightly open,
I gasp at the thought that I created such beauty.
My heart can hardly contain this love, it feels like breaking
when all along it has been mending.
You have given me the biggest love I will ever feel,
you have given me a purpose,
as I gave you the breath of life, you have given me the breath of love
I used to write about the big things.
Not realising that these are the big things.
You are.
You.
You are worth writing about.

Butterflies

Butterflies are not always
a sign of love and connection.
Seek the one that makes your heart
calm and at peace,
and you might just find
your home.

Passing ships

Tell me who you are,
and why you have entered my life.
Tell me about all the things you have done
whilst we've been apart.
Are you going to take my hand
and walk with me for a while?
Are you going to unveil my soul?

Tell me,
are you here to stay?
Or are we going to be
passing
ships
in the ocean of
life?

Falling

What if I told you I was falling for you,
that my heart was beating differently?
What if I told you that I missed you,
that I needed you?
What if I told you I was falling for you?
Would you be there to catch me?

You'll break it

He is there, simply there.
He reaches out with another perfect sweet kiss.
His hands at the bottom of my neck slowly tracing my face.
He smells of fresh summer breeze.
He doesn't talk much, yet his eyes tell me a thousand stories
of love and hope,
of passion and tenderness.
He is there, giving me the space to wander.
He sees my walls and breaks them down one by one.
And for a short while, I know I want to allow him to do just that.
To see me for who I really am.
Hoping it will be enough,
praying I won't run,
trying not to break anything.
This time.
'It won't last - fear whispers - you'll mess it up'.
Defeat and sorrow:
what else could there be in such
perfection?

All or nothing

Love me ferociously,
hungrily, softly.
Love all the parts of me
that scare you to death.
Love my darkness
as much as my light.
Love me as I am,
or
not
at
all.

Fantasy and reality

There is an abyss between fantasy and reality.
Says the hiker at the bottom of the mountain,
says the bird about to fly for the first time,
says the lover in despair.
All you need is one leap,
one flap of the wings,
one breath.

The beginning

We will begin at the beginning.
We will scan the perimeter of our hearts
like animals do in a new territory.
We will go slow,
we will sniff each other and our past,
we will stare at each other for hours,
not moving, but studying, dancing slowly around each other.
We will not let hunger dictate how fast we will feast
on each other.
How can we describe these feelings if not with the simple
words we don't say?
But our lives are complete already, balanced, full.
To let you in is to open a door,
one I can't go back to closing quickly.
So I leave it ajar as I study the colour of your soul.
As I listen for hours to all the books you've ever written.
To your dreams and fears.
I will listen to listen, not to respond.
I will study how your eyes roll when you're about to say
something difficult,
and how your body twitches when your voice cracks
with emotions you don't want to show.
How you stop to look at me when I get my hair up,
how your gaze locks into mine
as you rest your head on your folded arms on your desk
and slowly look up to look at me.

As if you've never seen anything so beautiful in all your life.
In that moment when you feel all the emotions your heart is capable of, all your efforts are in not saying anything.
We will begin at the beginning,
we will make love to each other's minds before a finger is laid on each other's bodies.
We will learn our stories and what our souls crave.
We will be. Simply be who we are. Who we always were.
Raw and authentic, we will tell each other the truth.
Like the ocean and its salt, the truth will burn on the raw flesh we are exposing to each other.
Until the old skin falls off, we will kiss the scars
and wait for new skin to grow, healed, new, virgin.
We will begin at the beginning,
until it will become the middle,
and eventually the end.
The end of the search for the truth,
for love, for the last sunset.
Because you will be my new beginning,
and I will be your
last
ending.

Someone I could love

You feel like someone
I could love
endlessly and delicately,
like a slow sunset
giving way to the stars.
Where the darkness
this time
is only there to treasure
our secrets
and deepest desires.

The siren's call

Can you hear the ancient siren's song?
The sweet notes that permeate your soul,
filling your heart with warmth.
The siren is calling for you
through mountains and valleys,
oceans and rivers,
through this life and the next.
She is the enchantment you never thought
you'd fall for;
she is the light in the night.
Answer the damn call.
She is everything you ever wished for.

A new chapter

You are something else,
a different chapter.
A new book,
blank pages still to be written.
It has my name on it,
it has our name.
I want to be the ink spilled on those pages.

I need you

All I need is a soft embrace,
no, not just a hug and simply touching.
I need you to embrace
my racing mind, my broken heart,
my endless thoughts.
Until I feel safe again,
until I can breathe again.
Can you do that?

Be with you

'If you could do anything to make you smile
right now, what would it be?'
he asked softly.
The answer was so simple,
it came out even before her next breath did.
It was like a lullaby, an enchantment,
a spell reciting:
'Be with you, be with you'.

Feeling safe

Walk with me,
on the path of a million contradictions,
of impossible futures
and hopeless dreams.
It's the safest I have ever felt.

What you could be

Talk to me again
about how the sunrise moves you,
of the flames burning inside
waiting for the right heart to set on fire.
Of a future made of moonlight walks
and caramel coffees.
Of bodies moving together pulling each other's
souls in,
fusing in perfect harmony
in a world of chaos
where everything finally
makes sense.
Let us become.
I am already in love
with everything you could
become to me.

Breath of fire

I am everything
you are afraid to
surrender to,
for my love knows
no limits.
I am the breath
of fire you have
never
known.

Sugar and honey

I dreamt about sugar and honey,
about fire and ice,
the opposites and the equals.
Lost in the memory
of your sweet scent,
passion in my heart,
quiet in my soul,
I woke up with your name
  on
    my
      lips.

Strange comfort

There is a strange comfort
when I am around you.
A surreal feeling of
knowing, of finally
'being'.

Firefly in a jar

I wish I could bottle up this feeling
like putting a firefly in a jar.
So I could open it up
every time I miss you,
and remember the feeling
of flying free
whilst being held
  tighter
    than
      ever.

Me and you

Me, you, and time.
That's ALL I need.

Falling in love

There is nothing that I love more
than to fall in love:
with a new song,
a poem,
an idea,
a dream,
and you...
over and over again.

New language

I need a new language to translate
into words your silences.
How many
I love yous
are hidden in the way you look at me?

Intimacy

Intimacy is a slow dance in the kitchen,
a reassuring look in a crowded room.
It's a 2am call answered by 'are you okay' instead of 'hello'.
It's belly laughter at the most ridiculous thing.
It's passing by each other on a busy morning
and still brushing your hand on my face.
It's knowing when to hold me for a bit longer after a hard day.
It's having those difficult conversations
knowing we are safe and honouring our truth.
It's saying 'you're mine' whilst leaving the freedom
to navigate on our own,
knowing we will always find each other
in the only place that is safe:
our hearts.

Kiss me a little longer

Kiss me a little longer,
through the lines of my poems;
ask the wind to play
with my hair, just like you would.
Tell the Earth to hold me tight,
till you can do so.
Ask the fire to keep me warm tonight,
till I am in your arms:
the only place
I
long
to
be.

A new chaos

You and I
are a different
definition of love.
A new language,
a different kind of
chaos.

I want to belong

I want to be that song
you escape to,
the tree that grows
with the seeds of trust,
the flower that blossoms
with drops of love.
I want to be the earth
you watch all your sunrises on.
I want to belong,
belong to us.

In your arms

There is nothing I want more
than to collapse into your arms.
To finally sleep for all the nights
I didn't.
To hear those comforting words
I have been missing for so long.
To open my heart knowing
I am safe.
To finally rest,
to finally breathe.

Listen with your heart

Ask me how I am,
not what I have done today.
Ask me about what I am feeling,
what I am afraid of,
and truly listen to my answers.
I don't need solutions,
I don't need fixing.
If you don't really see me,
all you'll ever hear
is just the sound of my voice,
never the true melody
of my heart.

Trust

When I say I need to trust you,
I don't simply mean trust that you will be faithful.
I need to trust that you'll listen to me
when I need to repeat things over and over to process them.
Trust that you'll keep my heart safe,
trust that you will honour our truth
and keep an open heart.
Trust that you won't run away when things get tough,
trust that you will hold me tighter on the nights
I feel the weight of the world,
trust that you will let me wander in depths of my own mind
when I need space,
Trust that you will ride the waves of my contradictions without judgment,
Trust that you will see beauty in my scars
and love me more for each of them.

Everything that is good with the world

'What do you see in me
when you look at me so sweetly?'
she asked with sleepy eyes
waking up to his loving gaze.
'Everything that is good about the world',
he replied as he held her
a bit closer to his chest.

Shelter

Talk to me, my love,
whisper softly what you
have been afraid to say.
Feel your lungs
expanding, burning
as you finally allow some oxygen in.
I will give your words shelter,
I will keep them safe.
You can breathe now,
I will keep you
safe.

Colours

Spill colours into my soul,
paint away that grey;
only you can carve out
the rainbow
buried
by a thousand black shadows.

Scars

Breathe in my scars,
bleed red blood at every
sharp edge you try to smooth.
Break down these walls,
with love and gentle whispers.
Magic is found in broken pieces
finally, once and for all,
back together.

A new horizon

I want to drink bitter coffee and make sweet love,
I want kisses at midnight and morning silences,
I want to stare in your eyes
and look for the buried galaxies,
I want to create the safety for them
to be out in the broad light.
I want to give oxygen to this love,
I want the fire to start,
I want the flames surrounding us to burn down the past,
I want everything that is real and raw.
I want the impossible,
the one that brings me to my knees,
and I want to do it together,
like children running
with big dreams in their pockets
burned ground behind them,
a new horizon ahead.

Pink sunset

I will always meet you
in that little space
between the morning light
and the sweetest of sunsets,
smiling at the sight
of our souls dancing together,
at last reunited
after many lifetimes.

Shadows

I love the darkness in you,
it makes my shadows
more bearable.

Equal passion

I can't explain why I love you,
just like I can't explain why
I love watching a raging flame.
I must have an equal passion
for everything
    that
        burns.

Naked

All I want is to be naked with you,
which has little to do with being without clothes.
I want to show you my bare soul,
all the parts of me I keep hidden in the darkness,
all those parts that make me think
I am unlovable.
All I want is for you to see me,
deep down,
no masks,
no pretending.
I want you to set my heart on fire
and reach the core of the flames,
unburnt, unscathed,
dancing together
in a forever melody
that no-one else can hear.

Surrender to love

This love doesn't feel like a choice anymore,
rather an inevitability
to surrender to.
Is love really a choice?

Constellations

Open that door that you have kept closed
for so long, my love.
Show me all the constellations
and how our planets align.
I can see a new universe
coming through,
as the light is so bright.
Let's get lost
in the magic of new beginnings,
leaving any fears outside,
we don't need it here.
The universe has a different notion
of time and space,
nothing is as it seems,
and yet everything is exactly
how we feel it.
So, I will be here waiting.
Find me where the stars fall,
and catch me,
every time.

Your name

Your name was always engraved
in my heart
even before the beginning of time.
I carried it with me
through the flames of hell,
the storms, and the oceans
of all the lives we ever lived,
and all the ones we ever will.
Other bodies, different eras,
new sunrises,
not knowing who we were,
finding each other yet once again.
And after the last sunset
this earth will ever see,
my love,
your name will be the only sweet echo
my soul will whisper

one last time

to the dying stars.

Raw truth

I don't want small talk
I don't care about the weather or if you like to play sports.
I want to know what's behind the mask,
I want to have a soul conversation.
Raw, unfiltered.
Give me the truth,
the blood and bones,
give me depth,
give me something real.
Give me passion.
Set my soul on fire,
reach me
where no one else
ever could.

Always yours

Come a little closer,
let me in your world slowly,
as we breathe in the gentle breeze of change
and look at the colours
of new beginnings.
Let me explore like a child
looking at the beauty of a caterpillar
that becomes a butterfly.
Our worlds, already perfectly balanced and complete,
collide like stars.
Come a little closer,
hear my words echoing
in the stardust surrounding us:
I have always been yours.

Love is madness

Madness is taking hold of me,
I won't let go,
I'm in.
You are the voice I want to hear,
yours are the last eyes I want to see when
I fall asleep.
I don't want my name to fall on
anyone else's lips.
You are,
you were,
you always will be
what my heart has been craving.
Madness is now a crystal-clear thought.
Feel me there,
in your heart,
right where I belong.

Faith

And when they will ask me
why did I wait,
why did I hold on for eons?

I will simply reply:
'My faith was stronger.'

Nothing is ever
 truly
  lost.

Just us

I call in everything that is pure and real,
I long to give you the purity of my heart,
I call in the passion this body
is burning to give you,
the fibres of my being wanting to fuse with
yours into forever.
I call in our love, now.
This is where we are supposed to be.
the past is behind us,
broken pieces flying away.
Breathe, my love,
the universe is cocooning us.
We are exactly where we are supposed to be.

The only space between us

When longing meets reality,
in a space that is only ours,
I can feel your heart beating
as you gently trace your fingers in my hair;
the silence is telling us a million stories,
we honour it by listening
to our souls talking the ancient language
of love,
the one spoken with no words.
After all the lives we have lived apart,
my love,
how beautiful it is when the only space
between us
is now
just
our
breath.

Acknowledgments

I would like to thank Gabrielle G for her guidance, support and friendship - this book wouldn't be here today without her.

To Beth Spary, for being on my journey again and creating the amazing illustrations of this book.

To Stefanie Briar, who edited the book and encouraged me to carry on.

A special thank you to my brother Emmanuel for creating the beautiful format of this book, and to Tom for his careful proofreading.

To my family and friends for continuing to believe in me, and my beautiful daughters who are the reason I write - I am so lucky to have you in my life.

And a very special thank you to my readers and all the Instagram community, your support means the world to me.

About the Author

Barbara Gianquitto is a poet, writer and author of the bestselling poetry collection *4:04AM Thoughts*.

Barbara writes about love and heartbreak, self-discovery and healing. Her soft, open and unique voice has gathered the interest of over 30 thousand readers on social media across the world and BBC national radio.

As a graduate in communication and psychology, Barbara has a passion for the power of words, inspiring her readers to dive deeper into their own power and self-discovery.

Born and raised in Italy, Barbara currently lives in the United Kingdom with her family and two grumpy cats. She drinks far too much coffee, follows the Moon and all its phases and is a hopeless romantic.

You can find more about Barbara's work and upcoming projects at www.barbaragianquitto.com.

Words are all we have in this world.

We should use them more often

@barbara.gianquitto.author

@BarbaraNgianquitto

@bgianquitto

@barbara.gianquitto

Index

Printed in Poland
by Amazon Fulfillment
Poland Sp. z o.o., Wrocław
29 June 2022

744a1bdd-e4fa-4f99-921b-1b9f3cf4506cR01